Questions and Answers: Countries

Germany

by Kremena Spengler

Consultant:
James J. Sheehan
Professor of History
Stanford University
Stanford, California

Capstone
press

Mankato, Minnesota

Fact Finders is published by Capstone Press
151 Good Counsel Drive, P.O. Box 669, Mankato, Minnesota 56002
www.capstonepress.com

Library of Congress Cataloging-in-Publication Data
Spengler, Kremena.
Germany / by Kremena Spengler.
p. cm.—(Fact finders. Questions and answers: countries)
Includes bibliographical references and index.
Contents: Where is Germany?—When did Germany become a country?—What type of
government does Germany have?—What kind of housing does Germany have?—What are
Germany's forms of transportation?—What are Germany's major industries?—What is
school like in Germany?—What are Germany's favorite sports and games?—What are the
traditional art forms in Germany?—What major holidays do people in Germany celebrate?—
What are the traditional foods of Germany?—What is family life like in Germany?
ISBN 0-7368-2690-4 (hardcover)
1. Germany—Juvenile literature. [1. Germany.] I. Title. II. Series.
DD17.S54 2005
943—dc22   2003026873

Editorial Credits
Megan Schoeneberger, editor; Kia Adams, series designer; Jennifer Bergstrom, book designer;
maps.com, map illustrator; Wanda Winch, photo researcher; Scott Thoms, photo editor;
Eric Kudalis, product planning editor

Photo Credits
AP/Wide World Photos/Jan Bauer, 22–23
Art Directors/TRIP/Martin Barlow, 21
Beryl Goldberg, 16–17, 19, 25, 27
Capstone Press Archives, 29 (top)
Corbis/Brooks Kraft, 9; Premium Stock, 13; Royalty Free, 1
Folio Inc./Walter Bibikow, 4
Getty Images Inc., 15
Photodisc Inc./John Wang, 10–11; Mel Curtis, cover (background)
StockHaus Limited, 29 (bottom)
SuperStock, 7; Steve Vidler, cover (foreground)

Artistic Effects
Ingram Publishing, 12, 24; Photodisc/C Squared Studios, 16 (bottom)

1 2 3 4 5 6 09 08 07 06 05 04

Table of Contents

Features

Where is Germany?

Germany is a country in north-central Europe. It is a little smaller than the U.S. state of Montana.

Mountains are an important landform in Germany. Part of the Alps mountain chain stretches along Germany's southern border. This area has tall peaks and many lakes.

A road winds through the Alps mountain chain in southern Germany. ➤

Legend

⊛ Capital

• City

🌲 Forest

⛰ Mountain Range

〜 River

Scale

| 0 | 100 | 200 Miles |

| 0 | 100 | 200 Kilometers |

DENMARK

Baltic Sea

North Sea

NETHERLANDS

Hamburg

POLAND

Berlin ⊛

GERMANY

Elbe River

Rhine River

Cologne •

BELGIUM

CZECH REPUBLIC

LUXEMBOURG

• Frankfurt

FRANCE

Black Forest

Danube River

Munich •

Alps

AUSTRIA

SWITZERLAND

Germany also has forests and rivers. The Black Forest in southwestern Germany has many dark fir trees. Long rivers flow through the country. The Rhine, Elbe, and Danube are major German rivers.

When did Germany become a country?

Germany first became a country in 1871. Until then, Germany was divided into separate states. One state, Prussia, became powerful. In 1871, its leader, Otto von Bismarck, joined the states together. Bismarck became Germany's first **chancellor**. William I was the **emperor**. Emperors ruled Germany from 1871 to 1918.

After World War I (1914–1918), Germany became a **republic**. From 1933 to 1945, it was ruled by Adolf Hitler and the Nazi Party.

Fact!

In 1961, East German leaders built a wall through the city of Berlin. They wanted to stop people from traveling to West Germany. The Berlin Wall was removed in 1989.

Otto von Bismarck was the first leader to unite Germany.

In 1949, Germany split into two countries, West Germany and East Germany. They had separate leaders and laws. East Germany and West Germany united to become one country again on October 3, 1990.

What type of government does Germany have?

Germany is a **federal republic**. In this form of government, several states are united under a single leader. The states also have their own leaders. They can make their own laws. Germany has 16 states.

Germany has two main leaders. The president is the head of Germany. The president represents Germany at important events. The chancellor runs the country.

Fact!

The United States is also a federal republic.

The German parliament meets in the Reichstag building in Berlin.

Germany's **parliament** meets in the capital city of Berlin to make laws. It has two groups, the Bundestag and the Bundesrat. The people elect members of the Bundestag. The states name leaders to join the Bundesrat.

What kind of housing does Germany have?

Most Germans live in apartments or houses. High-rise apartment buildings are common in large cities. In smaller towns, Germans live in one-story or two-story town houses. More than half of Germans rent their homes.

Where do people in Germany live?

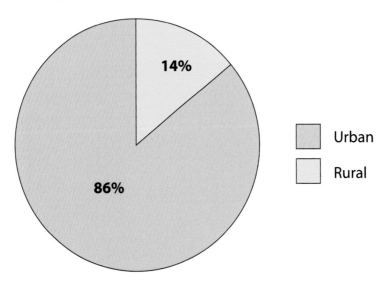

14%

86%

Urban

Rural

Houses in cities are often built close together.

Housing in what was East Germany is more run-down than housing in the west. Many of the houses are older and smaller. Since 1990, Germans have worked hard to improve these homes and build new ones.

What are Germany's forms of transportation?

Germany has more roads than any other country except the United States. Trucks carry most goods across the country. Car travel is also very popular. Germany has superhighways called autobahns. Many of these roads have four or more lanes.

Germany also has good railroads. About half of the lines are electric. High-speed trains connect major German cities. The trains travel at about 160 miles (260 kilometers) per hour.

Fact!

Bicycles are popular in Germany. Most cities have a separate lane for bicycles next to the sidewalks.

Trucks and cars travel on Germany's superhighways, called autobahns.

German airports connect to about 300 cities in more than 100 countries. Frankfurt's airport is one of the world's busiest airports.

What are Germany's major industries?

Germany makes most of its money in **manufacturing**. German factories make machines, tools, chemicals, electronics, and ships. They also make cloth and foods. Germany also makes many cars. Mercedes, BMW, and Volkswagen are famous German cars.

Most people work in Germany's service industries. Banking, real estate, and tourism are some of the service industries in Germany.

What does Germany import and export?

Imports	Exports
food products	cars
metals	chemicals
textiles	machinery

German factories use computers to build cars.

Farming is a small part of the **economy**. Farmers raise livestock for milk and meat. They grow wheat, oats, and sugar beets.

What is school like in Germany?

Up to fourth grade, German schools are like U.S. schools. After fourth grade, German students choose one of three kinds of schools.

Some children go to secondary schools, or *hauptschule*. They study language, math, and science for five or six years. Afterward, they train for jobs.

Some children go to intermediate schools, or *realschule*. These schools offer more business and foreign language classes. The program lasts six years. Students then go to business schools.

Fact!

On the first day of school, German parents give first graders a big colorful cardboard cone full of candy and school supplies.

Students at a German gymnasium study many subjects.

Other children go to grammar schools, or gymnasium, to prepare for college. They study languages, math, and science. These schools last nine years.

17

What are Germany's favorite sports and games?

Soccer is Germany's most popular sport. Millions of Germans play it. Many towns and cities have teams. During soccer season, thousands of Germans watch weekly pro games.

Many Germans are members of sports clubs. At clubs, people play soccer, tennis, handball, volleyball, and basketball.

Fact!

German figure skater Katerina Witt won two Olympic gold medals.

Germans in-line skate through the streets of Berlin.

Recently, in-line skating has become popular in Germany. Most big cities have "blade nights." They close the streets to cars so people can skate safely.

What are the traditional art forms in Germany?

Germany's classical music is well known around the world. Johann Sebastian Bach, Georg Friedrich Handel, Ludwig van Beethoven, and Richard Wagner are among the world's most famous composers. Today, Germany has many fine orchestras.

Fact!

Builders began working on the Cologne Cathedral in 1248. The building was finished in 1880.

Germans have built beautiful churches and castles. The Cologne Cathedral in Cologne is known for its tall towers. The Neuschwanstein Castle in southern Germany was built between 1869 and 1886. More than 1 million people visit the castle each year.

What major holidays do people in Germany celebrate?

Germans celebrate many holidays. December 6 is St. Nicholas Day. The night before, children put their shoes by the door. In the morning, children find candy in their shoes. Germans spend New Year's Eve with friends and family. At midnight, fireworks go off, and church bells ring. Many Germans also celebrate other holidays, such as Easter and Christmas.

What other holidays do people in Germany celebrate?

Ascension Day
Harvest Festival
Labor Day
May Day

Large crowds gather in front of the Brandenburg Gate in Berlin to celebrate Unity Day.

Germans celebrate their national holiday on October 3. This holiday, called Unity Day, started in 1990. It marks the day when East Germany and West Germany became one country again.

What are the traditional foods of Germany?

Germans make 1,500 kinds of sausages. German sausages, called wurst, are world famous. Germans eat sausages with rolls at breakfast and at other meals.

Germans eat a lot of meat. One popular dish is breaded fried pork called schnitzel. Germans also like beef, chicken, and turkey. Some Germans eat goose on Christmas.

Fact!

Germans from the city of Hamburg called cooked ground beef "Hamburg steak." In the 1880s, many people from Hamburg moved to the United States. Their Hamburg steaks became known as hamburgers. Americans added buns later.

German shops sell many kinds of meat and sausages.

Potatoes and cabbage are popular side dishes. Potatoes are boiled, fried, mashed, or made into pancakes. Germans boil cabbage and mix it with **vinegar** to make sauerkraut.

What is family life like in Germany?

In Germany, some parents take off work to be with their young children. German parents can take three years off from work. The family receives money from the government to help pay bills. Most parents return to work when their children are older.

What are the ethnic backgrounds of people in Germany?

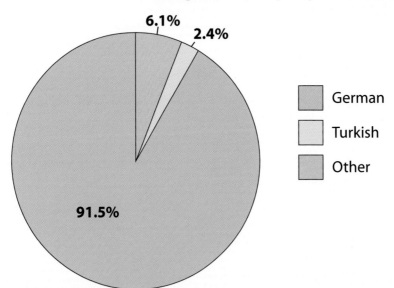

6.1%

2.4%

91.5%

German

Turkish

Other

Many German children use cell phones to talk to friends and family.

German children are very busy. Children often meet their friends in cafes, parks, or at youth clubs. Most German children talk to friends on cell phones, which they call "handys." They also play computer games.

Germany Fast Facts

Official name:

Federal Republic of Germany

Population:

82,398,326 people

Land area:

134,835 square miles
(349,223 square kilometers)

Capital city:

Berlin

Average annual precipitation:

27.5 inches (70 centimeters)

Language:

German

Average January temperature:

48 degrees Fahrenheit
(9 degrees Celsius)

Natural resources:

coal, iron ore, wood

Average July temperature:

90 degrees Fahrenheit
(32 degrees Celsius)

Religions:

Protestant	34%
Roman Catholic	34%
Islamic	3.7%
Other	28.3%

Money and Flag

Money:

Germany's money is the euro. In 2004, 1 U.S. dollar equaled .8 euro. One Canadian dollar equaled .6 euro.

Flag:

The German flag has equal stripes of black, red, and gold. These colors stand for German unity.

Learn to Speak German

People in Germany speak German. It is the official language. Learn to speak some German using the words below.

English	German	Pronunciation
hello	hallo	(HAHL-oh)
good day	guten tag	(GOOT-un TAHG)
good-bye	auf weidersehen	(OWF VEE-der-zay-en)
yes	ja	(YAH)
no	nein	(NINE)
thank you	danke	(DAHNK-uh)

Glossary

chancellor (CHAN-suh-lur)—a title for the leader of a country

economy (i-KON-uh-mee)—the way a country runs its industry, trade, and finance

emperor (EM-pur-ur)—the ruler of an area called an empire

federal republic (FED-ur-uhl ri-PUHB-lik)—a government of many states led by a president or prime minister with officials elected by voters

manufacturing (man-yuh-FAK-chur-ing)—the process of making something

parliament (PAR-luh-muhnt)—the group of people who have been elected to make laws in some countries

republic (ri-PUHB-lik)—a government with officials elected by the people; republics are often headed by presidents.

vinegar (VIN-uh-gur)—a sour liquid used to flavor and preserve food

Internet Sites

FactHound offers a safe, fun way to find Internet sites related to this book. All of the sites on FactHound have been researched by our staff.

Here's how:
1. Visit *www.facthound.com*
2. Type in this special code **0736826904** for age-appropriate sites. Or enter a search word related to this book for a more general search.
3. Click on the **Fetch It** button.

FactHound will fetch the best sites for you!

Read More

Gray, Shirley. *Germany.* First Reports. Minneapolis: Compass Point Books, 2002.

Gray, Susan Heinrichs. *Germany.* A True Book. New York: Children's Press, 2003.

Tecco, Betsy Dru. *How to Draw Germany's Sights and Symbols.* A Kid's Guide to Drawing the Countries of the World. New York: PowerKids Press, 2004.

Index